STAR WARS™

THE FORCE AWAKENS

ULTIMATE STICKER COLLECTION

HOW TO USE THIS BOOK

Read the captions, then find
the sticker that best fits the space.
(Hint: check the sticker labels for clues!)

•

Don't forget that your stickers can be
stuck down and peeled off again.

•

There are lots of fantastic extra
stickers for creating your own
scenes throughout the book.

 Penguin Random House

Written and Edited by David Fentiman
Project Art Editor Owen Bennett
Creative Technical Support Tom Morse
Senior Pre-production Producer Jennifer Murray
Senior Producer Alex Bell
Managing Editor Sadie Smith
Managing Art Editor Ron Stobbart
Art Director Lisa Lanzarini
Publisher Julie Ferris
Publishing Director Simon Beecroft

For Cameron + Company
Designers Dagmar Trojanek, Amy Wheless and Jillian Lungaro
Creative Director Iain Morris

For Lucasfilm
Executive Editor Jonathan W. Rinzler
Image Archives Stacey Leong
Art Director Troy Alders
Story Group Leland Chee, Pablo Hidalgo and Rayne Roberts

First published in Great Britain in 2015 by
Dorling Kindersley Limited
80 Strand, London, WC2R 0RL
A Penguin Random House Company

10 9 8 7 6 5 4 3 2 1
001–288368–December/2015

Page design copyright © 2015 Dorling Kindersley Limited

© & TM 2015 LUCASFILM LTD.

A CIP catalogue record for this book is available from the British Library.

ISBN 978-1-40933-660-0

Printed and bound in China

A WORLD OF IDEAS:
SEE ALL THERE IS TO KNOW

www.dk.com
www.starwars.com

A NEW AGE

Many years ago, a great war raged across the galaxy. The stories tell of a brave rebellion against an evil Empire, and the heroes who fought for freedom. But that was all a long time ago, and now the galaxy has entered a new and darker age.

The First Order

The First Order is all that is left of the evil Galactic Empire. The Empire was defeated and destroyed 30 years ago, but now it has risen again, and it wants revenge!

The Resistance

The Resistance is the only thing that stands between the First Order and control of the galaxy. It is led by General Leia Organa.

The New Republic

The New Republic replaced the Empire after the war and now rules the galaxy. It has become corrupt and weak, and doesn't believe that the First Order is a threat.

Kylo Ren

Kylo Ren is a fearsome warrior who fights for the First Order. Kylo uses a laser sword known as a lightsaber, and a mysterious power known as the Force.

General Leia

General Leia leads the Resistance. Many years ago, she and her brother, Luke Skywalker, helped to defeat the Empire. Now Leia fights to stop the First Order, but Luke has vanished.

Han and Chewbacca

Han and Chewbacca are smugglers who have flown together for a very long time. They were once heroes of the Rebellion, but they have since gone back to their old criminal ways.

Finn

Finn was raised as part of the First Order. His real name is FN-2187. He was trained as a stormtrooper, but he realises that the First Order is evil and he runs away.

Jakku

Jakku is a barren desert planet. There was once a big battle here, and now the world is covered with wrecked starships and abandoned vehicles.

Rey

Rey grew up on Jakku, and works as a scavenger in a junkyard. She does not realise it, but she can use the Force. She lives alone, and wishes she had a family to care for her.

REY ON HER SPEEDER

JAKKU

Jakku is a desert planet in the Western Reaches of the galaxy. It is a harsh, bleak place. No one would live here at all if it wasn't for the piles of valuable wreckage that cover its surface – all that remains of a great battle, a long time ago.

Lor San Tekka
Lor San Tekka is a great explorer who lives on Jakku. He owns a mysterious artefact that the Resistance and the First Order both want very badly.

Villagers
Lor San Tekka lives in a sacred village near the Kelvin Ravine. The villagers choose to live in the wilderness so they can focus on their religion.

Lor´s artefact
General Leia sends her most daring pilot, Poe Dameron, to collect this artefact from Lor. It is a clue to finding her missing brother, Luke Skywalker.

Luggabeast
Luggabeasts are cybernetic creatures. They wear armour on their heads, so no one really knows what they look like!

Teedo
Teedo is a small, grumpy creature who searches the desert looking for junk. He rides a mount known as a luggabeast.

Sand creature

This hungry sand creature keeps most of its body hidden beneath the dunes. It raises its eyes like a periscope to spot its prey, and then attacks it from below.

Sinking Fields

The Sinking Fields are very dangerous. Quicksand covers the whole area, and anyone foolish enough to wander into them will quickly disappear.

LOR SAN TEKKA

Starship Graveyard

Many years ago, during the war against the Empire, there was a huge battle above Jakku. The wreckage from the battle still litters the planet.

Niima Outpost

Niima Outpost is home to many scavengers. They travel out into the Starship Graveyard to salvage bits of technology, and then bring them back to trade.

REY

Rey has lived alone on Jakku for many years. She works in the junkyard as a scavenger, so she has become a genius with technology. Rey is also an amazing pilot, but her most impressive skills are ones that she doesn't even know she has!

REY AT NIIMA OUTPOST

Scavenger outfit
Scavenging is dangerous. The desert is home to hungry creatures and wrecked ships are full of sharp, broken machinery. Rey wears special clothes to protect herself.

Old helmet
Rey doesn't trade everything she finds in the wreckage. She keeps some things for herself, such as an old rebel pilot's helmet that she likes to wear.

Rey´s speeder
Rey rides an unusual speeder that she built herself. It is basically a huge engine with a small seat at the back. It looks hard to steer, but Rey makes it seem easy.

Wrecked ship
Rey is good at reaching remote spots that other scavengers can't. The inside of a giant wrecked Star Destroyer is an opportunity too good to miss!

Saving BB-8
Outside her house, Rey finds the droid BB-8 being kidnapped by a creature known as Teedo. She saves BB-8, but then he starts following her around!

Quarterstaff
Rey carries a large quarterstaff on her back to defend herself with. She is a skilled fighter, but she does not realise that her quick reflexes come from the Force.

Rey´s house
Rey's house is actually a wrecked vehicle, too. It is an old Imperial craft known as an AT-AT, which has fallen on its side.

Rey and Finn
When Rey first meets Finn, he is wearing Poe Dameron's pilot jacket, so she thinks he is a member of the Resistance. They run away from the First Order's troopers together.

Plucky pilot
Rey and Finn find the *Millennium Falcon* abandoned on Jakku, and use it to escape from the First Order. Rey's pilot skills mean they can outrun the ships that chase them.

NIIMA OUTPOST

Niima Outpost is the biggest town on Jakku.
Its shabby huts and tents are built out of scrap
from the junkyard. Niima is a dusty, unfriendly place.
Many of its residents are trapped here, working
for cruel junk dealers in return for tiny rations of food.

Niima citizens
Many different kinds of
people live in Niima. There
are humans, droids and
lots of aliens, too. They
all wear thick clothing to
protect themselves from the
hot desert sun.

Steelpecker
Steelpeckers are animals
with big, strong beaks.
Their name comes from their
diet of junk! They use their
beaks to break up wreckage
and then eat the metal.

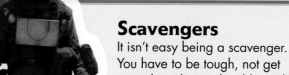

Scavengers
It isn't easy being a scavenger.
You have to be tough, not get
scared inside spooky old wrecks,
and know the difference between
worthless junk and a priceless find.

Bobbajo
Bobbajo is a
crittermonger.
He carries
creatures in
cages on his
back, and
sells them in the
marketplace.

Happabore
Happabores are massive, strong
creatures, but they are not dangerous.
They are used to drag heavy pieces
of wreckage across the desert.

Quadjumper

Quadjumpers are a type of starship docked at Niima Outpost. They have four huge engines, and look very fast.

Cleaning salvage
Rey brings her salvage to Niima Outpost to clean it. She then gives it to her boss, Unkar Plutt, in exchange for tiny portions of food.

Constable Zuvio

Constable Zuvio is part of the Niima Outpost Militia. This is a police force that watches for troublemakers and keeps the peace.

NIIMA OUTPOST

Unkar's henchmen

Mean junk dealer Unkar Plutt always keeps some goons close by, just in case he needs to boss anyone around.

THE RESISTANCE

General Leia's Resistance force is the only thing that can stop the First Order. The Resistance is small, and does not have many ships or weapons, but its members are brave, and they are determined to defend the galaxy.

Admiral Ackbar

Admiral Ackbar is one of Leia's commanders. He was also an admiral during the war against the Empire. Leia knows that she can rely on him.

Resistance base

The Resistance has a secret base in the Ileenium system, on a planet named D'Qar. This is where they plan their missions.

Poe Dameron

Poe is Leia's greatest pilot. He always volunteers for the most dangerous missions, and he leads the other Resistance pilots into battle.

The General

Leia leads the Resistance as its general. Her soldiers have all heard stories about her bravery and wisdom. They will follow her without a second thought.

BB-8

BB-8 is Poe's astromech droid. He helps Poe fly his X-wing, plot courses through space and make repairs to his ship.

Aliens and droids

Lots of different alien species have joined the battle against the First Order. There are also droids, who arm and repair the Resistance's ships.

Admiral Statura

Admiral Statura is Leia's second-in-command. He is good at planning missions, and knows a lot about weapons and technology.

ADMIRAL ACKBAR

Resistance pilots

The Resistance has many brave pilots. They fly X-wings and are led by Poe Dameron. They include Ello Asty, Nien Nunb, Snap Wexley and Jess Pava.

X-wings

X-wings are small, fast ships. They can attack other ships or targets on the ground. The Resistance's X-wings are more advanced versions of ships used by the old Rebel Alliance.

THE FIRST ORDER

The evil First Order has risen from the ashes of the Galactic Empire. It has kept itself hidden for years while it built up its strength, but now it is ready to strike. Its powerful fleet and legions of soldiers will try to conquer the galaxy!

GENERAL HUX

Stormtrooper
Stormtroopers are the First Order's soldiers. They are raised to fight from a very young age, and follow orders without question.

Dark enforcer
Kylo Ren is the champion of the First Order. Luke Skywalker trained him to be a Jedi, but he fell to the dark side of the Force and became evil. His Force powers make him incredibly strong and fast.

Interrogator droid
The First Order often questions its prisoners to get information. For this, it uses interrogator droids. These are designed to cause terrible pain without injuring their victim.

First Order officer

The First Order has many low-level officers who try to keep things running smoothly. It's a stressful job, and they always get the blame when things go wrong!

TIE fighter

TIE fighters are the First Order's main combat ships. They are fast and very agile. The old Empire invented TIE fighters, but the First Order has upgraded them.

First Order technician

The First Order's giant starships don't fly themselves! Thousands of skilled technicians keep the shields on, the engines running and the weapons firing.

General Hux

General Hux leads the First Order's military. He is an intelligent and ruthless commander. Hux is in charge of building the Starkiller superweapon.

The Starkiller

The Starkiller is a giant weapon with the power to destroy a whole star system! The First Order plans to use it to take over the galaxy. It is strongly shielded and nearly invincible.

TIE pilot

TIE fighter pilots are trained to destroy their enemy at all costs, even if that means sacrificing their own lives. They are deadly opponents.

KYLO REN

Kylo Ren is the First Order's greatest warrior. He wears a dark cloak and a mask, and carries a red, vicious-looking lightsaber. He shows no mercy to his enemies, and destroys anyone who opposes him.

KYLO REN

Star Destroyer

Kylo's Star Destroyer is named the *Finalizer*. It is a huge mobile base, and carries thousands of stormtroopers.

Kylo's mask

Kylo Ren wears a mask that covers his face. It is meant to frighten his enemies and keep his identity a mystery.

Interrogating Poe

Kylo Ren knows that Poe Dameron has hidden the artefact he needs. He uses the Force and an interrogator droid to make Poe reveal where it is.

Vader's helmet

Kylo admires Darth Vader – a Sith Lord who died many years ago – and keeps Vader's burned helmet in his room.

Kylo's lightsaber

Kylo's lightsaber is very unusual – it has three blades instead of one, and looks more like an ancient sword. It crackles and sparks when Kylo ignites it.

Shuttle

A special shuttle transports Kylo from his Star Destroyer to planets or other ships. It has huge wings and very powerful shields.

Kylo in battle

Kylo can use his lightsaber to slice through almost anything, and he can freeze blaster bolts in mid-air using the Force. Only someone who can use the Force will stand a chance against him.

STORMTROOPERS

Stormtroopers are the soldiers of the First Order. They are trained to be ruthless warriors, and to always follow orders. The old Empire had legions of stormtroopers, but those of the First Order are even more deadly!

Stormtrooper transport
Stormtroopers are carried into battle in special transport ships. These can travel through space and drop stormtroopers straight into combat.

Captain Phasma
Captain Phasma leads the First Order's stormtroopers. She wears special silver armour and a black cape. Phasma does not care about destroying innocent people.

Snowtrooper
The Starkiller has been built on a cold, icy planet. The stormtroopers there have been given special cold weather uniforms to protect them from the freezing temperatures.

Phasma´s rifle
Like her armour, Captain Phasma's blaster rifle has a special silver coating. She is one of the best shots in the whole First Order!

New armour
First Order stormtroopers look a lot like those of the Empire from decades ago, but their armour has been updated and they carry new, advanced weapons.

Megablaster

When stormtroopers have to destroy big targets, they use heavy weapons like the megablaster. Megablasters are bulky and hard to use, but they pack a big punch.

Riot gear

Some stormtroopers are specially trained for close combat. They carry shields and menacing energy batons, and are very dangerous.

Flametrooper

Flametroopers are armed with deadly flamethrowers that can burn down a building in seconds. They wear extra armour to protect themselves from their weapons.

FINN

Finn was raised by the First Order. He was trained as a stormtrooper, but in his first ever battle he realises that the First Order is evil, and he refuses to fight. He manages to escape from the First Order with Poe Dameron, and ends up at Niima Outpost.

FINN ON JAKKU

Stormtrooper Finn
With his stormtrooper armour on, Finn looks just like thousands of other stormtroopers. When he runs away, he has to change out of it as fast as possible!

Battle on Jakku
Finn's first battle is on Jakku. When the stormtroopers are ordered to wipe out innocent villagers, Finn refuses, and decides to run away.

Rescuing Poe
Finn wants to escape from the First Order, but he needs a pilot to get away. He rescues Poe from his cell on Kylo Ren's Star Destroyer, and together they steal a TIE fighter.

Crash site

Poe and Finn's stolen TIE fighter crashes in the Sinking Fields, in the Goazan Badlands. Finn barely escapes before the ship is swallowed up by quicksand.

Disguise

Finn and Poe's TIE gets shot down and crashes on Jakku. Afterwards, Finn can't find Poe in the wreckage, but he finds Poe's jacket. He puts it on to hide his stormtrooper uniform.

Happabore trough

Finn walks from the crash site to Niima Outpost through the scorching desert. When he arrives, Finn is so thirsty he drinks from a happabore's water trough, but he quickly regrets it!

On the run

When Rey and BB-8 are being chased by stormtroopers, Rey sees Finn and thinks that he is a member of the Resistance. She grabs him and they escape together.

Gunner Finn

Rey and Finn escape from Jakku in the *Millennium Falcon*. While Rey pilots the ship, Finn jumps into the gunner's position.

GENERAL LEIA

Leia was part of the Rebel Alliance that defeated the old Galactic Empire. She fought bravely in many battles. When the First Order rose from the ruins of the Empire, Leia formed the Resistance to defend the galaxy. She is now searching for her brother, Luke Skywalker.

GENERAL LEIA

Leia in uniform

Leia grew up as a princess, but she abandoned the clothes and jewels of royalty a long time ago. Most of the time she wears a uniform, just like her soldiers.

Korr Sella

Korr Sella is Leia's representative in the New Republic government. She tries to convince the Republic Senate to fight back against the First Order.

R2-D2

R2-D2 was once Luke Skywalker's droid. He joined Luke on many adventures, and helped him in many battles. When Luke vanished, R2-D2 stopped talking to anyone.

C-3PO

Like R2-D2, C-3PO was once owned by Luke Skywalker, and he took part in the war against the Empire. As a protocol droid, C-3PO has served at Princess Leia's side for decades.

Leia's blaster

Leia has always been a great shot. Even though she is now the commander of the Resistance, she always carries a blaster pistol to defend herself with.

Republic senators

The New Republic is no longer a symbol of law and democracy – over the years it has become weak and corrupt. Many of the senators don't trust Leia.

HAN AND CHEWIE

Han Solo and his co-pilot Chewbacca were once heroes in the Rebellion against the Empire. Han was a smuggler who joined the rebels and then fell in love with Princess Leia. In the years since the war, Han and Chewie have gone back to a life of smuggling.

Han Solo

Han was a great general in the Rebellion. He flew many dangerous missions, and saved Leia's life many times. He is famous across the galaxy.

The *Millennium Falcon*

The *Millennium Falcon* was once Han and Chewie's ship. They flew it in battles against the Empire, but they lost it after the war. They have been searching for it ever since.

Han and Leia

Han and Leia fell in love, and after the war against the Empire was won, they got married. Even though tragedy has since driven them apart, they still care for each other deeply.

Chewie's bowcaster

Chewie uses a Wookiee bowcaster as his weapon. It fires a powerful energy bolt that can punch through thick armour.

Chewbacca

Chewbacca is a Wookiee. Wookiees are extremely strong and brave warriors. Chewbacca owes his life to Han, and will never leave him.

Han´s blaster
Han has carried this blaster pistol for decades. It is old-fashioned, but Han thinks it is lucky, so he will never replace it.

HAN AND CHEWIE ON BOARD THE *MILLENNIUM FALCON*

GANGSTERS

During their many years of smuggling, Han and Chewie have made a lot of enemies in the galaxy's criminal underworld. It's only a matter of time before some of these gangsters join forces to try and get revenge!

BALA-TIK

Kanjiklub

The scruffy Kanjiklub have joined the hunt for Han and Chewie. They are very dangerous, and have a reputation for stealing starships.

Guavian Death Gang

The Guavian Death Gang are well known across the galaxy for their advanced weapons, red armour, combat training and ruthlessness.

Kanjiklub weapons

Unlike the Guavian Death Gang, the members of the Kanjiklub all have different equipment. Some of their blasters look old and worn, but they can still do serious damage!

Bala-Tik

Bala-Tik is a leader in the Guavian Death Gang. His bosses lent Han some money, but when they realised Han wasn't going to pay them back, they sent Bala-Tik to hunt him down.

Guavian weapons

The powerful blaster rifles carried by the Guavian Death Gang are highly illegal, but Republic laws don't reach this remote part of the galaxy.

Tasu Leech

Tasu Leech is leader of the Kanjiklub. Even his own gang members are scared of him! He has been challenged as leader many times, but he always destroys his rivals.

Razoo Qin-Fee

Razoo Qin-Fee is Tasu Leech's lieutenant. He is a weapons expert who repairs and upgrades the gang's equipment.

TASU LEECH

Tasu Leech's blaster

Tasu Leech is highly skilled in hand-to-hand combat. His blaster has a built-in bayonet blade, so he can fight his enemies up-close.

POE DAMERON

Poe is General Leia's best starfighter pilot. He is very brave and always volunteers for the most dangerous missions. He commands the Resistance pilots of Blue and Red squadrons, who all admire his courage and combat skills.

Poe's jacket

Poe is very attached to his flying jacket. When Poe goes missing, Finn borrows the jacket to replace his own stormtrooper uniform.

Flight gear

Poe wears a Resistance pilot's uniform. It looks like the old uniforms of the Rebel Alliance, but it has been updated with a new helmet.

Trusty droid

BB-8 is Poe's loyal astromech droid. Astromech droids are robots that help pilots fly their starships. BB-8 has a modern design – his head stays still while his body rolls underneath!

Poe's X-wing

As the Resistance's top pilot, Poe is allowed to fly his own special ship. It is an X-wing coloured black and orange.

SF TIE fighter

After Poe gets captured, he steals a Special Forces TIE fighter to escape from Kylo Ren's Star Destroyer. It is larger and better armed than a normal TIE fighter, and has two pilots.

Quadnoculars

Poe carries a trusty pair of quadnoculars with him on missions. They let him see great distances, so he can see danger coming from a long way away.

Poe captured!

Poe flies to Jakku to get an important artefact from the explorer Lor San Tekka. Unfortunately Poe gets captured by Kylo Ren, but he gives the artefact to BB-8, who manages to escape.

MAZ'S CASTLE

Maz Kanata is one of the most famous pirates in the galaxy. Her castle on the planet Takodana is a haven for smugglers, gangsters and pirates from every corner of space. Some are just here to have fun, but others have much more sinister plans.

CAPTAIN ITHANO

Maz's guests

It seems that no two aliens in Maz's castle look the same. Maz's guests come from all over the galaxy. There are species here that even Han and Chewie have never seen before!

Bazine Netal

Bazine is really a spy for the First Order. When Finn and Rey arrive at the castle, she tells the First Order that they are there.

Grummgar

Grummgar is a big, tough brute, who will smash anyone who looks at him the wrong way. He only really cares about two things: fighting and hunting.

Pirate crew

Finn has second thoughts about joining the Resistance, and tries to join a crew of pirates instead. He changes his mind again when he sees Rey in trouble.

GA-97

The Resistance has its own spy in Maz's castle. This droid has a direct link to C-3PO, and when he spots BB-8 with Finn and Rey, he contacts the Resistance.

Castle cook

Maz has a lot of guests to feed, with a lot of different tastes. Her cook tries to keep things simple – roasted meat is popular with most species.

Use the extra stickers to create your own scene.

STICKERS

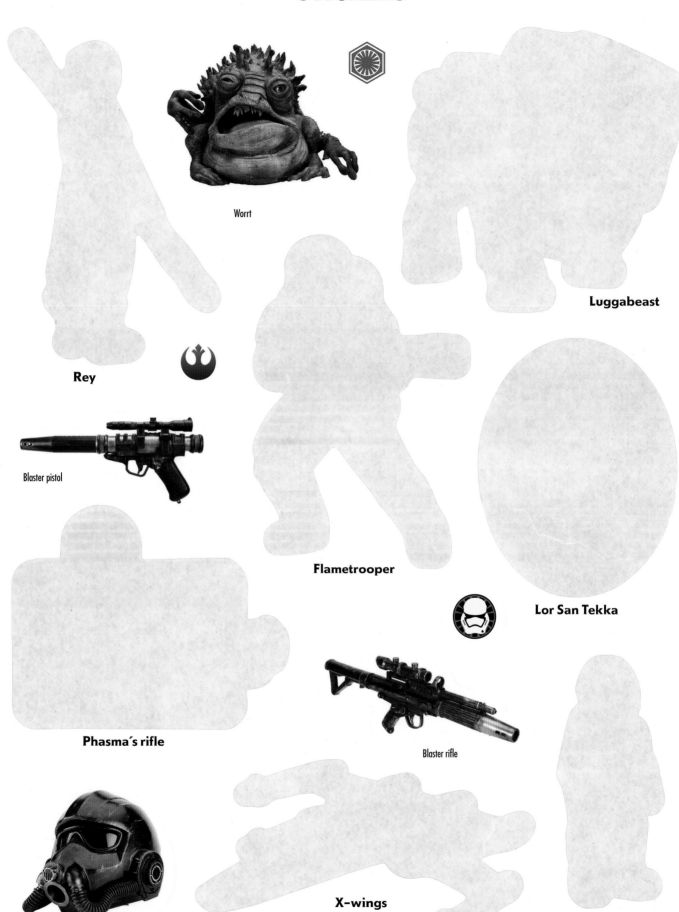

Worrt

Luggabeast

Rey

Blaster pistol

Flametrooper

Lor San Tekka

Phasma´s rifle

Blaster rifle

Smuggler helmet

X-wings

Aliens and droids

STICKERS

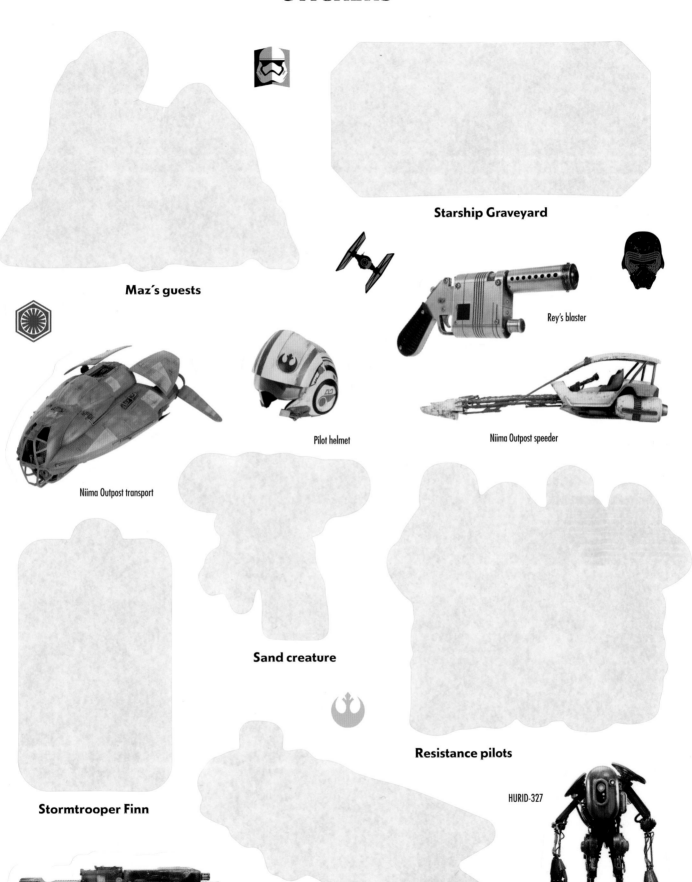

Maz's guests

Starship Graveyard

Rey's blaster

Niima Outpost transport

Pilot helmet

Niima Outpost speeder

Sand creature

Resistance pilots

Stormtrooper Finn

HURID-327

Advanced blaster

Stormtrooper transport

STICKERS

Poe's helmet

New armour

The *Finalizer*

On the run

Donderbus blaster

M9-G8

Grummgar

Razoo Qin-Fee

Scavenger outfit

Megablaster

Resistance base

The New Republic

Nien Nunb

STICKERS

Prize box

Rey´s
speeder

Brave Poe

Captain Phasma

Kanjiklub

Niima Outpost

Training remote

TIE pilot

Disguise

Castle cook

Niima militia

Mouse droid

Plucky Pilot

STICKERS

Battle on Jakku

Flamethrower

Admiral Ackbar

PZ-4CO

BB-8

The *Millennium Falcon*

Rusty speeder

First Order technician

Republic senators

Kylo Ren

Saving BB-8

STICKERS

Poe captured!

Game tokens

Vader´s helmet

RP-G0

Finn

Megablaster trooper

Guavian weapons

Han Solo

Wollivan

Leia´s blaster

Villagers

Korr Sella

The First Order

STICKERS

Admiral Statura

Gunner Finn

Sarco Plank

General Leia

Tasu Leech's
blaster

Rey's helmet

Steelpecker

Hidden blaster

Trusty droid

Bazine Netal

Kylo in battle

The General

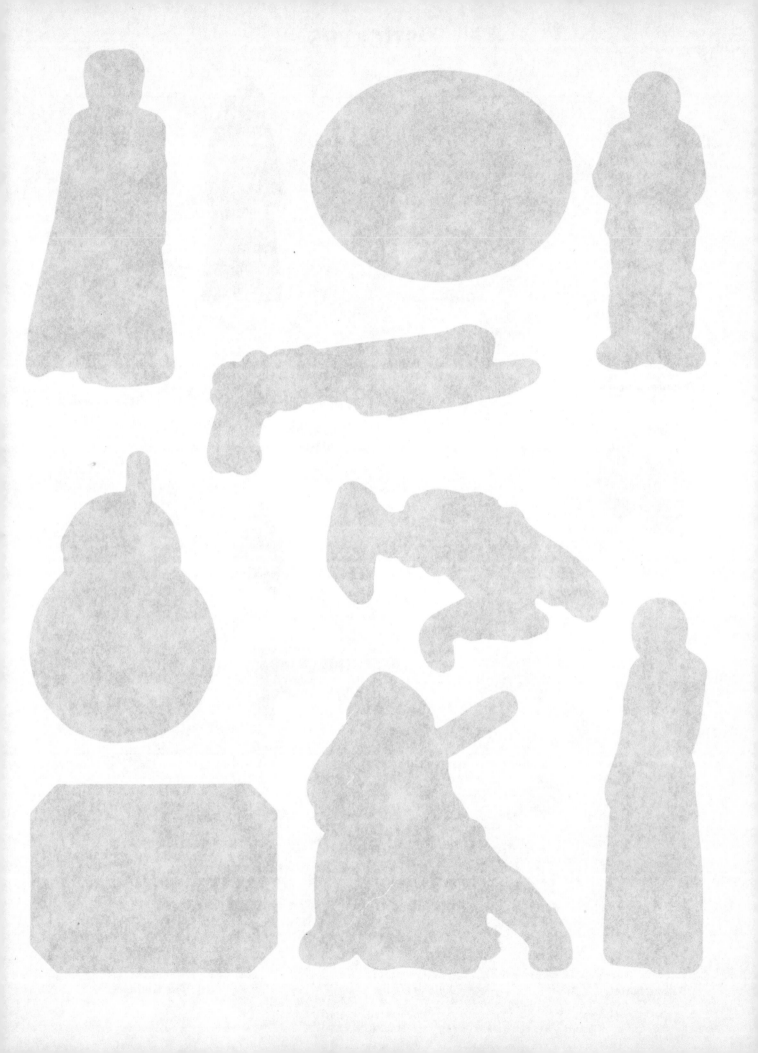

STICKERS

Teedo

Wrecked ship

B-U4D

Pamich Nerro

Flight gear

Junkyard minion

Han and Chewbacca

Interrogator droid

TIE fighter

Leia in uniform

Tusked alien

Bala-Tik

STICKERS

Han and Leia

Quarterstaff

Riot gear

Jakku

Hassk triplets

Kanjiklub weapons

Guavian soldier

Resistance Finn

Chromium blaster

Kylo´s mask

ME-8D9

First Order officer

Rescuing Poe

STICKERS

Happabore trough

Niima citizens

Scavengers

Quadnoculars

Protocol droid

Cleaning salvage

Pirate crew

Chewbacca

Ackbar in command

Winter warrior

R2-D2

STICKERS

SF TIE fighter

Happabore

Snowtrooper

Grey astromech

Interrogating Poe

Dark enforcer

Battered blaster

Bobbajo

Old helmet

GA-97

STICKERS

Sinking Fields

Poe´s X–wing

The Resistance

X-wings in action

General Hux

R2-D2 and C-3PO

Kylo´s lightsaber

GTAW-74

Tasu Leech

The Starkiller

Poe Dameron

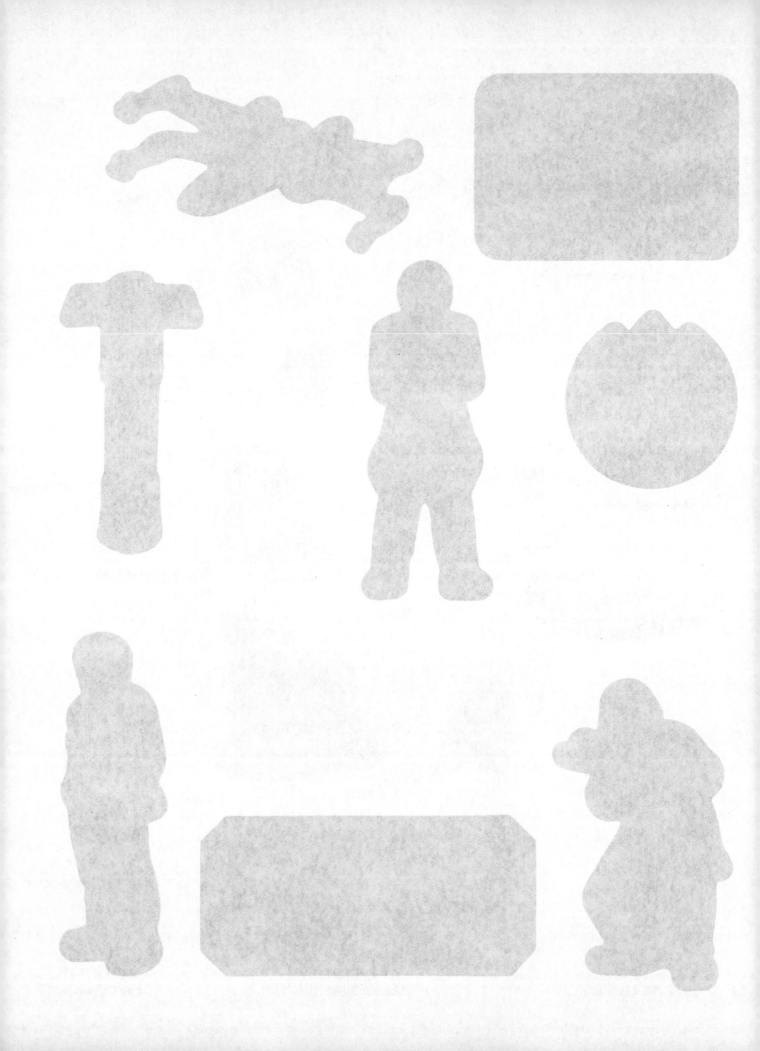

STICKERS

Crash site

Quadjumper

Old droid

Prashee and Cratinus

Rey´s house

**Guavian
Death Gang**

"Crusher" Roodown

Power droid

**Chewie´s
bowcaster**

Resistance astromech

Green pirate

Lor´s artefact   **Stormtrooper**   **Shuttle**

STICKERS

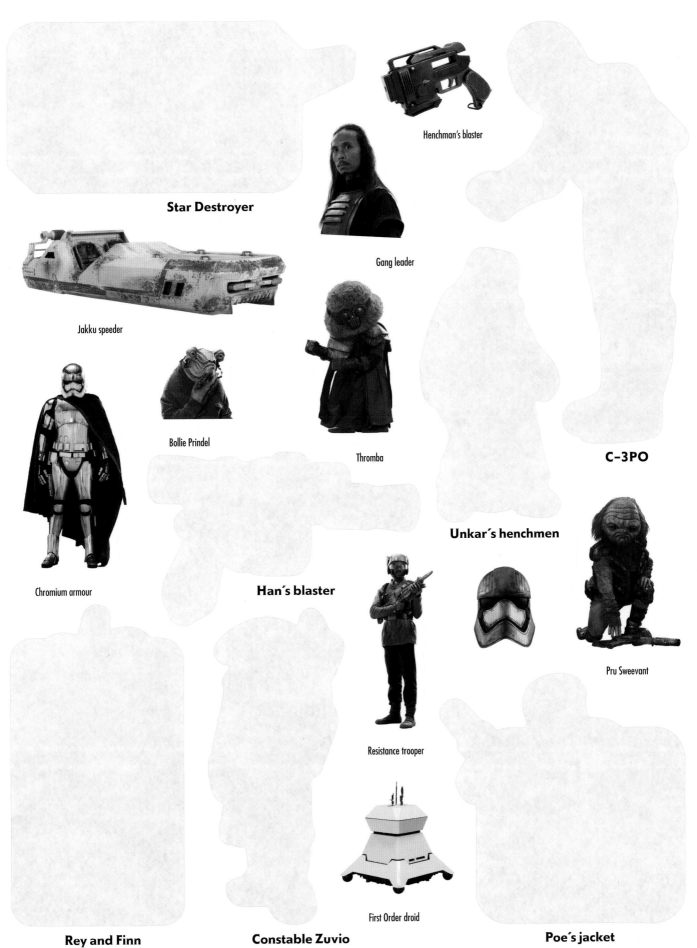

Henchman's blaster

Star Destroyer

Gang leader

Jakku speeder

Thromba

Bollie Prindel

C-3PO

Chromium armour

Unkar's henchmen

Han's blaster

Pru Sweevant

Resistance trooper

First Order droid

Rey and Finn

Constable Zuvio

Poe's jacket

STICKERS

STICKERS

EXTRA STICKERS

EXTRA STICKERS

EXTRA STICKERS

EXTRA STICKERS

EXTRA STICKERS

EXTRA STICKERS

EXTRA STICKERS

EXTRA STICKERS

EXTRA STICKERS

EXTRA STICKERS

EXTRA STICKERS

EXTRA STICKERS

EXTRA STICKERS

EXTRA STICKERS

EXTRA STICKERS

EXTRA STICKERS